Countries Around the World

Libya

Nick Hunter

W9-CLM-815

Heinemann Library
Chicago, Illinois

www.capstonepub.com
Visit our website to find out more information about Heinemann-Raintree books.

To order:
☎ Phone 888-454-2279

🖱 Visit www.capstonepub.com to browse our catalog and order online.

Edited by Abby Colich and Megan Cotugno
Designed by Philippa Jenkins
Original illustrations © Capstone Global Library, Ltd.
Illustrated by Oxford Designers & Illustrators
Picture research by Liz Alexander
Originated by Capstone Global Library, Ltd.
Printed in the USA

15 14 13 12 11
10 9 8 7 6 5 4 3 2 1

Library of Congress Cataloging-in-Publication Data
Hunter, Nick.
  Libya / Nick Hunter.
    p. cm.—(Countries around the world)
  Includes bibliographical references and index.
  ISBN 978-1-4329-6104-6 (hb)—ISBN 978-1-4329-6130-5 (pb) 1.
Libya—Juvenile literature. 2. Libya—History—Juvenile literature. I.
Title.
  DT215.H86 2012
  961.2—dc22   2011015431

Acknowledgments
We would like to thank the following for permission to reproduce photographs: Alamy: pp. 21 (© Oliver Gerhard), 22 (© Charles O. Cecil), 27 (© Paul Doyle), 29 (© John Warburton-Lee Photography), 32 (© MARKA); Capstone Global Library, Ltd.: p. 33 (Philippa Jenkins); Corbis: p. 25 (© John Van Hasselt); Dreamstime. com: p. 20 (© Igorj); Getty Images: pp. 8 (Rolls Press/Popperfoto), 15 (Reza), 17 (Benjamin Lowy), 19 (Bashar Shglila), 23 (Philippe Bourseiller), 31 (Reza), 34 (Marwan Naamani/AFP), 35 (Benjamin Lowy); iStockphoto: p. 13 (© AmandaLewis); Photolibrary: p. 30 (JTB Photo); Shutterstock: pp. 5 (© Pascal Rateau), 6 (© Pascal Rateau), 7 (© John Copland), 9 (© Pascal Rateau), 10 (© Mark III Photonics), 28 (© apdesign), 39 (© Styve Reineck), 46 (© Route66).

Cover photograph of gates leading to Old Medina's center, Tripoli, Libya, reproduced with permission from Photolibrary (Ken Scicluna).

We would like to thank Shiera S. el-Malik for her invaluable help in the preparation of this book.

Every effort has been made to contact copyright holders of material reproduced in this book. Any omissions will be rectified in subsequent printings if notice is given to the publisher.

Disclaimer
All the Internet addresses (URLs) given in this book were valid at the time of going to press. However, due to the dynamic nature of the Internet, some addresses may have changed, or sites may have changed or ceased to exist since publication. While the author and publisher regret any inconvenience this may cause readers, no responsibility for any such changes can be accepted by either the author or the publisher.

Contents

Some words are printed in bold, **like this**. You can find out what they mean by looking in the glossary.

Introducing Libya

Libya is a country of contrasts. Most of the North African country's people live in major cities along the long Mediterranean coast, but the Sahara Desert, which covers much of North Africa, dominates this vast and ancient country.

Ancient and modern

Libya's **economy** is largely based on its huge reserves of oil beneath the desert sands. The oil industry has made Libya a wealthy country. However, outside the main cities, many Libyan people raise animals the way they were raised centuries ago.

Despite the unchanging way of life for many of its people, Libya is a very modern country. Wealth from oil has helped to provide health care and education. The culture of Libya is based on traditional family and tribal groups—and strict following of **Islam**.

Troubled times

In 2011 many of Libya's people rebelled against the government of Colonel Muammar el-Qaddafi. The rebels took control of many Libyan cities but the government fought back, using the army and air force to attack its own people. In late 2011, Qaddafi was killed and the rebels began to form a new government. Many Libyans hoped that these dramatic events would make Libya more open to the outside world. Before the revolution, Libya had been a very isolated society.

YOUNG PEOPLE

Libya is a young country with a third of its population under the age of 15. Young people were at the heart of anti-government protests that erupted in 2011. Most young people have to do military service in Libya. Many also find it difficult to get jobs.

Libya is the fourth largest country in Africa. The shifting sands of the Sahara Desert cover much of the country.

History: Crossroads of Cultures

The first settlers probably came to Libya more than 10,000 years ago. Carvings and cave paintings tell us that the land was much greener than the desert landscape of today. The first people of Libya were probably **Berbers**, also called *Imazighen*. They gradually settled in small groups and became farmers. The people of ancient Egypt knew about the Libyans. In fact, kings from Libya ruled ancient Egypt from about 945 to 730 BCE.

Rock carvings like this one show that wild animals and plants flourished in Libya in prehistoric times.

Phoenicians and Greeks

Around 900 to 700 BCE, **Phoenicians** from the area that is now Lebanon began to trade along Africa's north coast. Trading posts were set up along the Libyan coast, including the city that would become Tripoli, Libya's modern capital. Ancient Greeks also settled the coast and set up the city of Cyrene, one of the most important centers for art and culture in the Greek world.

Roman Libya

In the first century BCE, Tripolitania, the region ruled from the Phoenician city of Carthage, and Cyrenaica, the Greek **colony**, came under the rule of ancient Rome. The Romans ruled the region for centuries and built great cities such as Leptis Magna.

The arrival of Islam

One of the most significant events in Libya's history was the Arab invasion in 642 CE. Muhammad, the founder of **Islam**, had died in 632 and quickly his followers spread their religion across most of North Africa.

The Roman city of Leptis Magna became one of the most beautiful cities of the **Roman Empire** during the reign of Emperor Septimius Severus (193–211 CE).

The Ottoman Empire

In the centuries following the arrival of Islam, the cities of the North African region known as the **Maghreb** (modern Libya, Tunisia, Algeria, and Morocco) were centers of learning and culture. Modern Libya is actually made up of three different regions. Tripolitania is in the northwest around Tripoli, with Cyrenaica to the east and Fezzan in the southern desert. In the 1500s, these regions became part of the Turkish **Ottoman Empire**.

Italian occupation and war

In the late 1800s, the Ottomans' power began to decline, and European countries invaded many African countries to rule them as part of their own **empires**. Italy invaded Libya in 1911. Italian rule was not popular. Nonetheless, by World War II (1939–1945), one-fifth of Libya's population was made up of settlers from Italy.

World War II changed everything. North Africa saw fierce fighting, and the Libyan city of Benghazi suffered more than 1,000 air raids as Allied forces tried to defeat German and Italian troops. After the war, the **United Nations** agreed to create a united country of Libya from the three regions of Tripolitania, Cyrenaica, and Fezzan.

Fighting in Libya during World War II destroyed many of Libya's buildings and roads.

UMAR AL-MUKHTAR (1862–1931)

Umar al-Mukhtar is revered as a Libyan national hero. He led a fierce **guerrilla** war against the Italian army in the 1920s. The Italians brutally punished anyone who sheltered the rebels. In 1931, Umar al-Mukhtar was captured and hanged in front of 20,000 people.

Centuries of Ottoman rule left their mark on Libya with buildings like this clock tower in Tripoli.

Independence

On December 24, 1951, King Idris I declared Libya an independent country. At first, the new Libya was friendly to **Western** countries, including the United States. With little wealth of its own, Libya relied on foreign aid.

All that changed in 1959 when oil was discovered in Libya. Libya was now able to survive on its own. Unhappy about the king's pro-Western policies, a group of army officers led by Colonel Muammar el-Qaddafi took power on September 1, 1969.

COLONEL MUAMMAR EL-QADDAFI
(1942-2011)

Colonel Qaddafi was the Arab world's longest serving leader and held total power in Libya until the rebellion of 2011. Born in a tent in the desert, he came to power at the age of 27. Qaddafi argued strongly for **unity** among Arab states and unity within Africa. His support for terrorist groups brought him into conflict with Western countries. U.S. forces bombed Libya in 1986, killing his adopted daughter. His brutal response to rebels in 2011 once again made him a villain in the eyes of many people. He was forced out of power during the Libyan civil war and killed in uncertain circumstances.

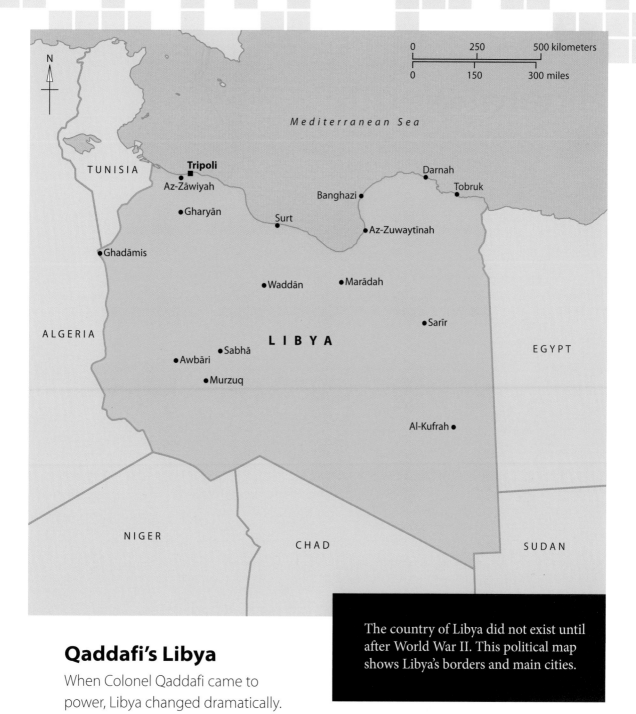

The scale shows:
0 — 250 — 500 kilometers
0 — 150 — 300 miles

Mediterranean Sea

TUNISIA

Tripoli
Az-Zāwiyah

Darnah
Tobruk

Banghazi

Gharyān

Surt

Az-Zuwaytīnah

Ghadāmis

Waddān

Marādah

ALGERIA

Sarīr

L I B Y A

EGYPT

Awbāri

Sabhā

Murzuq

Al-Kufrah

NIGER

CHAD

SUDAN

The country of Libya did not exist until after World War II. This political map shows Libya's borders and main cities.

Qaddafi's Libya

When Colonel Qaddafi came to power, Libya changed dramatically. Although Qaddafi was in power for more than 40 years, and Libya's people became wealthier than ever before, Libya's recent history has not been smooth. After an assassination attempt, Qaddafi created a large security network to reinforce his own power. This enabled Qaddafi to defeat anyone who dared to oppose his rule. However, in 2011, rebels who opposed the regime began fighting Qaddafi loyalists, and finally defeated them, after months of civil war.

Regions and Resources: Mineral Wealth

Libya is the fourth largest country in Africa. At 679,362 square miles (1,759,540 square kilometers), it is slightly larger than Alaska. Yet Libya has a population of only just over 6 million people. This means that there is a lot of land without people.

Libya has two main regions: the coastal strip along the Mediterranean Sea and the huge, empty Sahara Desert to the south. Libya shares borders with Egypt to the east, Sudan, Chad, and Niger to the south, and Algeria and Tunisia to the west.

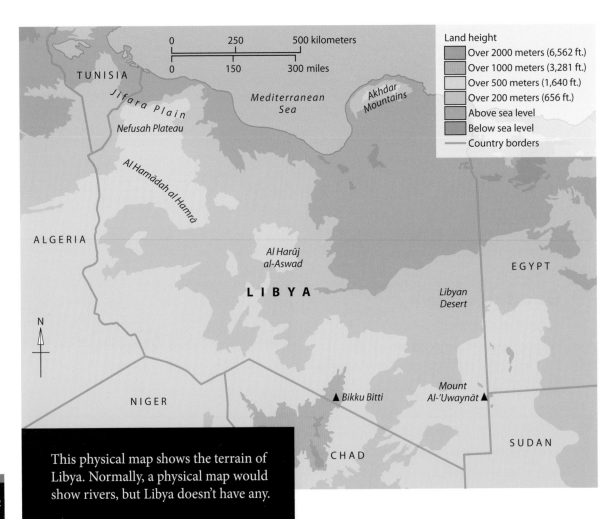

Land height
- Over 2000 meters (6,562 ft.)
- Over 1000 meters (3,281 ft.)
- Over 500 meters (1,640 ft.)
- Over 200 meters (656 ft.)
- Above sea level
- Below sea level
- Country borders

TUNISIA

Jifara Plain

Nefusah Plateau

Mediterranean Sea

Akhdar Mountains

Al Hamādah al Hamrā

ALGERIA

Al Harūj al-Aswad

LIBYA

Libyan Desert

EGYPT

N

NIGER

▲ Bikku Bitti

Mount Al-'Uwaynāt ▲

SUDAN

CHAD

This physical map shows the terrain of Libya. Normally, a physical map would show rivers, but Libya doesn't have any.

The only natural sources of water in the Sahara Desert are isolated oases where underground water comes to the surface.

Only a tiny amount of Libya's land is used for **agriculture**. This is mostly along the 1,100 miles (1,770 kilometers) of the Mediterranean coastal strip. Most people live in this area, too. The coastal plain rises up to the Nefusah **Plateau**. In the northeastern corner of Libya are the Akhdar, or green, Mountains.

Sahara Desert

Beyond these mountains, the desert takes over and covers about 90 percent of Libya. Almost nothing grows there—much is sandy with huge dunes that move with the wind. Farther south, the desert is more mountainous. Libya's tallest mountains are on the southern border with Chad.

Libya has no natural rivers. **Wadis** are dry riverbeds in the desert that fill up when it rains and then quickly run dry.

Weather and climate

Libya has a hot **climate**. Temperatures in the Sahara Desert typically reach more than 122°F (50°C). Desert temperatures fall dramatically at night because there are no clouds to keep warm air close to the ground. Deep in the desert, there is an average of less than 1 inch (25 millimeters) of rain each year. In some areas, it may not rain for several years. Near the Mediterranean coast, there is some rainfall, and temperatures are lower.

In the spring, the *ghibli* wind can raise violent dust storms in the desert regions. These can blow into the coastal strip, turn the sky red with dust, and raise the temperature to 122°F (50°C) for several days.

Water

With such a dry climate, lack of water is a problem. Beneath the Libyan desert are reserves of water. Some reserves have been brought to the surface and pumped to Libya's cities. Many believe this "Great Man-made River" project might eventually exhaust all Libya's water reserves and cause desert **oases** to disappear.

This chart shows the average rainfall and daily temperature for each month in Tripoli, Libya.

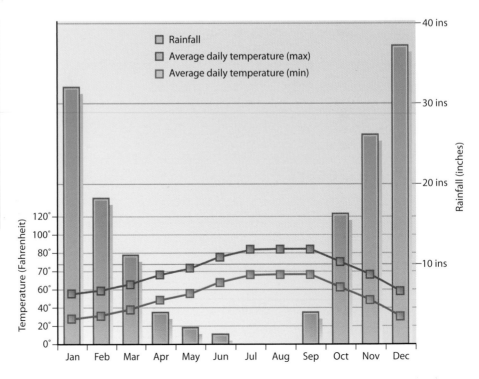

How to say...

Most people in Libya speak Arabic and so use a different alphabet from the one used in English. The following Arabic words are written as they would appear in the English alphabet:

sunny	*mushmis* (moosh-miss)	**rain**	*matir* (mah-tir)
hot	*harr* (hahrr)	**cold**	*barid* (bear-id)
storm	*asif* (a-sif)	**desert**	*sahra* (sa-ha-rah)

In a dust storm, strong winds lift tiny pieces of dust high into the air. The dust can travel hundreds of miles.

Economy

When Libya gained independence in 1951, it depended on foreign aid to keep its **economy** going. Today, Libya is the richest country in Africa. How did this happen? The answer is simple: oil.

Libya's economy is dominated by oil. Every country needs oil to run cars and airplanes, for example. Most countries have to **import** oil. Countries that have a lot of oil in the ground sell it to other countries and become very wealthy. Since oil was discovered in 1959, Libya has been able to build modern roads and cities with money from selling this essential **mineral**.

Libya has some of the world's largest **oil reserves** (see table on the next page). Most are located in the Sirte basin. Oil companies also believe there is more oil to be found in Libya. In addition to oil, Libya has large reserves of natural gas and smaller amounts of other minerals, such as iron and potash. Potash is used to make fertilizers that help crops grow.

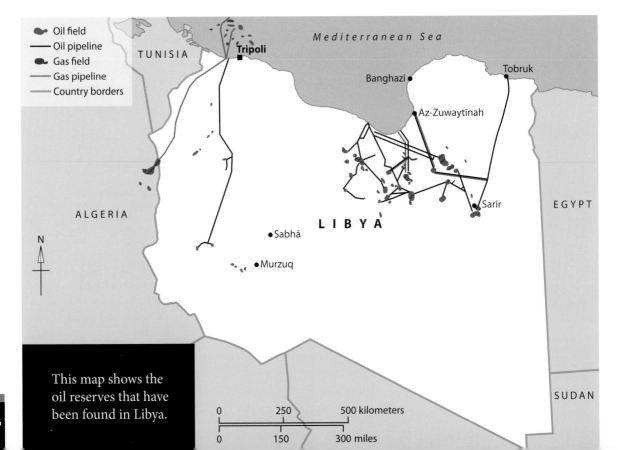

This map shows the oil reserves that have been found in Libya.

Facilities used by the oil industry were fought over by rebels and government forces in 2011.

Disadvantages

Oil has brought great wealth to Libya, but its effects have not all been positive. Libya's economy relies heavily on oil, and other industries have not really developed. If Libya's oil runs out, it would be a huge problem for the country.

Countries with the Largest Oil Reserves	Amount of Oil (in billions of barrels)
Saudi Arabia	264.6
Venezuela	172.3
Iran	137.6
Iraq	115.0
Kuwait	101.5
United Arab Emirates	97.8
Russian Federation	74.2
Libya	44.3
Kazakhstan	39.8
Nigeria	37.2

Source: BP Statistical Review of World Energy 2010

Other industries

Apart from industry related to oil, such as making oil drums, there is little industry in Libya. The **petrochemical** industry is also linked to oil. Products taken from oil are used to make everyday things—from plastic containers to cleaning fluids.

Food and farming

Before the discovery of oil, most of Libya's people farmed the land. However, Libya has never been well-suited to growing crops, and only 1 percent of Libya's land is used to grow food. Wheat, vegetables, olives, and some citrus fruits (such as oranges and lemons) are grown in a couple of regions.

Outside where crops are grown, **scrubland** has just enough **vegetation** for animals, such as goats and sheep, to feed. Elsewhere in the country, apart from around desert oases, there is not enough water to grow crops. Many foods are imported, and ambitious **irrigation** projects such as the "Great Man-made River" increase the area in Libya that can be farmed.

Daily Life

Although oil has brought wealth, it has not always brought jobs for the many people who have moved to Libya's cities. Around one in three people of working age in Libya do not have a job. This **unemployment** problem especially affects young people. When people do not have a job and cannot earn any money, they become unhappy. Libyans blamed the government for not providing enough jobs. High unemployment was one cause of protests against the government that led to the Libyan rebellion of 2011.

Migrant workers

Many workers move to Libya from elsewhere in Africa. Some stay in Libya and work in industry and farming. Others plan to save enough money to travel across the Mediterranean Sea to European countries, such as Italy and Malta.

Oil is plentiful in Libya, but water is a scarce and precious resource. This circle of crops in the desert is irrigated by water from deep underground.

Wildlife: Surviving in the Desert

Animals and plants need water to live, and the Sahara Desert is a difficult place for most animals to survive. According to ancient rock carvings, thousands of years ago lions, elephants, and giraffes were found in this region. But as the desert became drier and hotter, these animals were forced to move farther south.

Blending in

Large animals that are able to survive in Libya include gazelle and *waddan*. The *waddan* is also called the Barbary sheep, although it is more closely related to the goat. This sure-footed animal lives in rocky, dry areas and has adapted to its **habitat**. It can survive without water for an extended period of time. When threatened, the *waddan* stands completely still. Its sandy red color helps it to blend in with the surroundings. In the areas where the *waddan* lives, there is no **vegetation** to hide behind.

Dromedary camels can go without water for days. They sweat very little, and their body temperatures can increase by several degrees to survive in the heat. Today camels still carry goods across the desert—as they have for thousands of years.

Desert scorpions can survive at high temperatures, although they mostly move around at night.

Many non-mammals can survive in the desert. Reptiles, such as snakes and lizards, are **cold-blooded** creatures that rely on the heat of the sun to keep them alive. Even so, many, like the Sahara sand viper, bury themselves in the sand to protect themselves from the heat. They lie in wait for small mammals they might eat.

Plant life

Libya's coastal strip is rich in vegetation, including herbs, such as the asphodel. The only area of natural forest in Libya is on the northern edge of the Akhdar Mountains where cypress, juniper, and Aleppo pine trees face the sea and are sheltered from the heat of the desert.

Libya's Mediterranean coast and the Akhdar Mountains are very different from the desert that makes up most of the country.

How to say...

camel	*jamal* (ja-mahl)	**horse**	*hisan* (hi-sahn)
sheep	*kharuuf* (ka-roof)	**tree**	*shajara* (sha-ja-rah)
water	*ma'* (maya)	**flower**	*zahra* (zah-ra)

Away from the sea, some grasses grow in the areas of **scrubland**. Out in the desert, there is almost no vegetation. Only acacia trees provide shelter from the sun. These trees have very small leaves and long roots to capture any water they can. When occasional rains come to the desert, grasses will suddenly sprout up close to the **wadis**, dry ravines that briefly fill with water.

Desertification

The Sahara Desert is the world's biggest desert. It is about the size of the United States, and it continues to expand. Temperatures around the world are rising. This means that more places around the edges of deserts are becoming too hot and dry for plants to grow. Using underground water sources to **irrigate** crops adds to the problem. This **desertification** could affect Libya in two ways. First, it may mean that areas in Libya become even drier than they are now so that it is even more difficult to grow food. Second, people might move to countries such as Libya from south of the Sahara due to the growing desert.

Infrastructure: Dictatorship to Revolution

In 1977 Qaddafi wrote *The Green Book*, which set out Libya's political system. Qaddafi was officially called the Leader of the Revolution. For more than 40 years, he held almost all power in the country but in 2011 people across North Africa demanded change (see table).

Country	Political Change
Algeria	Widespread protests erupted against the government and rising food prices in 2011. President Abdelaziz Bouteflika promised to introduce **reforms**.
Egypt	President Hosni Mubarak resigned on February 11, 2011, after 30 years in power. A military government took over until new elections could be held.
Libya	In February 2011, many Libyans protested at the rule of Muammar Qaddafi, who responded by attacking his opponents with tanks and aircraft. The **United Nations** agreed to military action to protect Libya's people. Qaddafi was killed in October 2011.
Morocco	King Muhammad VI announced economic and political reforms following huge demonstrations in February 2011. The king controls many aspects of politics in Morocco.
Tunisia	President Zine al-Abidine Ben Ali stepped down in January 2011 following huge protests against his government. The new government has introduced democratic and legal reforms.

Mustafa Abdul Jalil, shown here, is the leader of the National Transitional Council of Libya. The Council represents the anti-Qaddafi rebels. The Council took over power in Libya in September 2011.

Under Qaddafi, Libya's people did not vote directly for the government as they would in a **democracy** like the United States. Each community had a local representative in the Libyan **parliament**, called the General People's **Congress**. The General People's Congress elected a committee to run the country, but important decisions were taken by Colonel Qaddafi.

The battle for Libya

In 2011 rebels took control of parts of Libya, particularly in the east around Benghazi. The rebels planned to "guide the country to free elections and the establishment of a constitution" once Qaddafi had been forced from power. The rebels finally defeated Qaddafi's forces and the dictator was killed. The National Transitional Council now has control of the country and hopes to stabilize the government.

Religion and the law

Religion is an important part of Libyan life. The country's laws are based on **Islamic**, or **sharia**, principles. They follow rules laid down in the Koran, the **Muslim** holy book

Living in Libya

The money Libya has made from oil has helped the Libyan people in many ways. Free health care and benefits, including pensions for the elderly, are provided—this is unusual for an African country. Education is also free for all Libyans.

Going to school

All Libyans have to go to school from age 6 to 15. Children attend elementary school for six years and middle and high school for three years each. About 80 percent of Libyans can read and write. Although girls and boys have equal treatment in the Libyan school system, families often do not send girls to school for very long. University education is also free for Libyans.

Sanctions

In the 1990s, Libya's people were negatively affected by trade **sanctions**. Other countries were banned from trading with Libya because of Libya's support of **terrorists**. After the sanctions ended in 2003, the government tried to improve Libya's **economy** but change was difficult because of the government's tight control of many parts of Libyan life and industry.

Rights and freedoms

Since 2003, Libya's government and people have been much more open to influence from other countries. Colonel Qaddafi's government, however, still controlled many aspects of life. Libyans did not enjoy many of the rights that people enjoy in most democratic countries.

When Libyans protested against the government in February 2011, they were arrested and attacked by Qaddafi's forces. Now the National Transitional Council is working to ensure the safety and liberation of all citizens.

Arabic is the primary language in school. Young people also learn English and have religious instruction.

Religion and the arts

Religion is at the center of Libyan life. The month of **Ramadan** is a key event in the Libyan calendar. During the month, **Muslims** fast, or do not eat, between sunrise and sunset. The festival of *Eid-ul-Fitr* at the end of Ramadan is a huge celebration.

Most Islamic art does not show images of people or animals, and this is also true of Libyan art. Folk arts include weaving, embroidery, and metalwork. The works featuring beautiful patterns and designs are often displayed in **mosques**, such as the Karamanli and Gurgi mosques in Tripoli.

Libya has many successful writers, but few are known outside the Arabic-speaking world. Much of Libyan writing has been concerned with politics. Under the Qaddafi regime, writers were not allowed to be critical, so much of the writing favored the government.

This tiled mosaic of a mosque in Tripoli is an example of traditional Libyan art.

Music and dance

Music is an important part of celebrations. Traditional music and folk dancing go together. Libyan music is played on instruments such as the *gheeta*, similar to a clarinet, and the *zukra* pipes. *Malouf* is often performed at weddings and involves a large group of musicians who sing and recite poetry about love or religion.

Folk dancing is common at Libyan festivals

Although there is a Libyan music industry, most pop music comes from Egypt, Tunisia, and Algeria.

IBRAHIM AL-KOUNI (B.1948)

Novelist Ibrahim al-Kouni's work is known across the Arab world and has been translated into many languages. Al-Kouni was born in the Libyan desert. His writing reflects his fascination with the Sahara Desert.

Food and shopping

Libyan food is much like the cuisine from the rest of North Africa. **Couscous** is part of many meals. Italian food has also had an influence. Pasta is the main ingredient in some dishes.

Family meals

Family meals are very important to Libyans. The family usually eats together unless there are guests. When guests are invited, men and women often eat separately. Before the main meal of the day, the family sits together, and water is passed around for hand washing. Everyone eats from a shared bowl, using only the right hand. In Libya, it is rude to use the left hand.

Libyan meals often have many courses, including spiced soups, salads, and main courses that mix meat with couscous or rice. In the cities, people buy food at the local *souq*, or market. Many Libyans also love sweets and pastries. Many small shops sell them. A traditional Libyan tea is often the last course of the meal.

Horse racing is a popular sport that often takes place on special days and holidays.

YOUNG PEOPLE

Soccer is the most popular sport in Libya. Tripoli and Benghazi are home to many of the top Libyan soccer teams. Young Libyans also follow Italian soccer. In fact, one of Colonel Qaddafi's sons briefly played for an Italian team. The African Cup of Nations is scheduled to be played in Libya in 2013.

Celebrations

Food is at the heart of many Libyan celebrations, such as weddings, which often last for several days.

Shaba Libiya (Libyan Soup)

Different variations of this soup are served at the beginning of many meals in Libya. Have an adult help you make it.

Ingredients

- 1 pound chopped stewing lamb
- 1 can chickpeas
- 1 chopped onion
- 2-3 tablespoons of tomato puree
- 1 tablespoon of dried mint or handful of parsley leaves
- spices including coriander, tumeric, and chilli powder
- 3 tablespoons of olive oil
- About 1 liter of water

What to do

1. Heat the oil and fry the onion until soft. Add the lamb, chickpeas, tomato puree and spices.
2. Cover the mixture with water and simmer for 35-40 minutes until the lamb is cooked.
3. Before serving, stir in dried mint or parsley.

Libya Today

Libya has seen many changes since the discovery of oil in 1959. Before oil was discovered, most Libyans lived outside cities. Today those cities are home to about 80 percent of Libyans. Despite huge political and economic changes, Libyans have kept many traditional parts of their way of life, based around **Islam** and family.

For many years, Libyans had little contact with other countries. The government's support for **terrorists** meant the country had few friends around the world. This was starting to change until Colonel Qaddafi's attacks on Libya's people after the protests in early 2011. People around the world condemned the Libyan leader and warplanes from many countries attacked Qaddafi's forces to protect the people of Libya.

Protesters wave Libya's flag in Benghazi on April 11, 2011.

The future

Libya's future is uncertain. Its new government faces many challenges. Libya's cities and oil industry have been badly damaged by the conflict. Many Libyans have also been forced to leave their country. After 40 years of being governed by Muammar el-Qaddafi, how will Libya adjust to a future without him?

Oil is vital to Libya's **economy** but our use of oil and other fossil fuels is causing climate change that could be particularly damaging to countries with a hot climate, such as Libya.

Fact File

Country Name: Libyan Republic

Capital: Tripoli (population: 2,189,000)

Language: Arabic, but Italian and English also spoken

Religion: Islam (97%), Other (2%)

Government: National Transitional Council overseeing move to democracy

National anthem: "Allahu Akbar" ("God is Greatest")

God is Greatest!
God is Greatest!
He is above the plots of the aggressors,
And He is the best helper of the oppressed.
With faith and with weapons I shall defend my country,
And the light of truth will shine in my hand.
Sing with me!
Sing with me!
God is Greatest!
God is Greatest!
God, God, God is Greatest!
God is above the aggressors.

Population: 6,461,454 (est. 2010)

Life Expectancy: 77.7 years (75.3 years for men, 80.1 years for women)

Bordering Countries: Egypt, Sudan, Chad, Niger, Algeria, and Tunisia

Total Land Area: 679,362 square miles (1,759,540 square kilometers)

Largest Cities: Benghazi, Al Hums, Az Zawiyah, Misratah, Zuwarah

Coastline:	1,100 miles (1,770 kilometers) along the Mediterranean Sea
Highest Elevation:	Bikku Bitti, 7,438 feet (2,267 meters), along border with Chad
Major Rivers:	No permanent rivers
Oil Reserves:	44.3 billion barrels
Other Natural Resources:	natural gas, gypsum
Currency:	Libyan Dinar = 1,000 dirhams
Unemployment Rate:	30%
Roads:	62,152 miles (100,024 kilometers); 35,551 miles (57,214 kilometers) paved

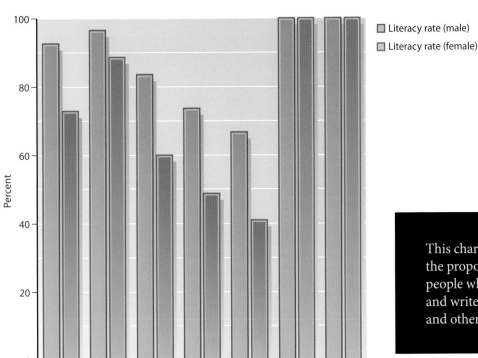

Literacy rate (male)
Literacy rate (female)

This chart compares the proportion of people who can read and write in Libya and other countries.

Famous Libyans: Ali Omar Ermes (b.1945), artist

Ahmed Fakroun (b.1953), musician

Mustafa Muhammad Abdul Jalil (b.1952), former Minister of Justice and leader of Libyan rebels' National Council

Ibrahim al-Kuoni (b.1948), author

Colonel Muammar el-Qaddafi (1942–2011), Libyan leader 1969 to 2011

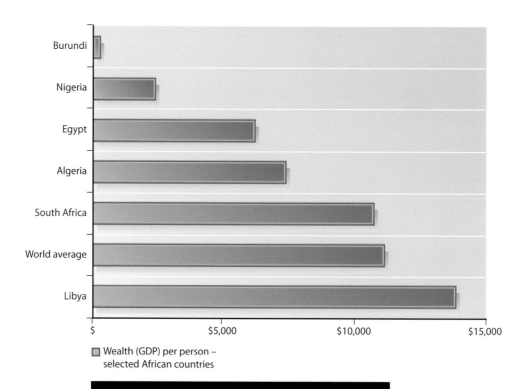

Wealth (GDP) per person – selected African countries

The value of everything produced in a country is called the Gross Domestic Product (GDP). Libya's GDP per person is higher than in other African countries, mainly because the country makes lots of money from oil.

Libya's UNESCO World Heritage Sites

World heritage sites must be outstanding examples of historical or natural interest. Libya's five world heritage sites highlight different parts of the country's history.

- **Cyrene**: center of ancient Greek civilization in Libya

- **Leptis Magna**: amazing ruins of a beautiful Roman city

- **Sabratha**: ruins of Phoenician trading post

- **Tadrart Acacus**: cave paintings that show the way of life in the Sahara up to 12,000 years ago

- **Old city of Ghadamès** (pictured below): example of an ancient Saharan city with traditional buildings

Ghadamès is one of the oldest towns in the Sahara region. The town's ancient buildings are clustered around a desert oasis.

Timeline

BCE is short for before the Common Era. BCE is added after a date and means that the date occurred before the birth of Jesus Christ, for example, 450 BCE.

CE is short for Common Era. CE is added after a date and means that the date occurred after the birth of Jesus Christ, for example, 720 CE.

BCE

c. 8000   Earliest evidence of settlements in Libya.

c. 1000   Phoenician traders establish trading posts on the Libyan coast.

63   Ancient Greek settlers found the city of Cyrene.

46   Julius Caesar adds Tripolitania to the Roman province of Africa; Cyrenaica and Tripolitania united in the first century CE.

CE

193   Septimus Severus becomes Roman emperor; Libyan city of Leptis Magna rebuilt and expanded.

642   Arab invaders begin to arrive in Libya, bringing Islamic faith.

1551   Ottoman Empire occupies Tripoli.

1911   Italy occupies Libya.

1942   Allied forces push Italians out of Libya, which is then divided into British and French regions.

1951   Libya declares its independence on December 24; King Idris becomes head of state.

1959   Oil first discovered in Libya.

1969   Military government led by Colonel Muammar el-Qaddafi takes over from the King of Libya on September 1.

1973   Qaddafi launches a "cultural revolution" creating people's committees in many workplaces and areas of society.

1975-1979   Qaddafi publishes three volumes of the *Green Book*, which sets out his ideas for the government of Libya.

1986   U.S. forces bomb Tripoli and Benghazi on April 15.

1988   On December 21, Pan Am flight 103 explodes over Lockerbie, Scotland, killing 270 people; Libyan man later convicted of causing the explosion.

1992   United Nations imposes sanctions on Libya, affecting Libya's trade and relations with other countries.

2003   United Nations sanctions lifted and Qaddafi promises to end development of chemical and biological weapons and stop support of terrorists.

2005   Qaddafi announces steps to modernize Libyan economy.

2009   Qaddafi becomes leader of the African Union; he calls for a "United States of Africa."

2010   European Union and Libya sign agreement on immigration.

2011   In February government troops fire on a protest in Benghazi following the arrest of a human rights activist. Protests spread across the country. A transitional government forms and an army of rebels fight Qadaffi's loyalists. Qadaffi is forced to leave power and go into hiding. The National Transitional Council takes over Libya's government. Qadaffi is killed in October 2011.

Glossary

agriculture farming; the production of crops or livestock

Berbers people, also called *Imazighen*, who lived in North Africa before the arrival, in the 600s CE, of Arab settlers from the east

climate general weather conditions over a long time, including temperature and precipitation, such as rain or snow

cold-blooded having a body temperature that changes with the environment

colony area controlled by a foreign country; usually, people from the foreign country live in the area

congress group of officials or representatives that meet to discuss issues

couscous cracked wheat, originally from North Africa, that is served with meat and vegetables

democracy form of government by the people or by the elected representatives of the people

desertification the process of fertile land becoming desert

dictatorship government by a ruler, or dictator, with total power who often takes power by force

economy management of the resources, finances, income, and expenses of a community or country

empire political unit that controls a very large area, usually broken into several separate countries or territories

guerrilla any armed group that is not part of a regular army, usually fighting against a larger force or invading army

habitat natural environment for a living being

import ship goods into a country from other nations

irrigate supply water to fields and land to grow crops

Islam religious faith of Muslims, based on the text of the Koran and teachings of the prophet Muhammad

Maghreb region of North Africa that includes Libya, Tunisia, Algeria, and Morocco

mineral substance that occurs naturally, including metals and oil

monarchy rule by a king or queen

mosque place of worship for Muslims

Muslim follower of Islam, or having to do with a follower of Islam

nomadic people who do not live in one place but move according to the season or to find grazing land for animals

oasis (pl. oases) fertile area in the desert where underground water comes to the surface

oil reserves oil that has been discovered underground but not yet brought to the surface

Ottoman Empire large empire based in the city of Constantinople (now Istanbul) that ruled much of the Middle East and North Africa from the 1200s to the 1900s

parliament group of people that makes and approves the laws of a country. In a democracy, the people elect the members of parliament.

petrochemical substances made by refining and processing petroleum or natural gas

Phoenicians ancient people from present-day Lebanon and southern Syria, who traded along the coasts of the Mediterranean Sea

plateau level area of land raised above the land around it

Ramadan month of fasting, from sunrise to sunset, during the Muslim year

reform change designed to improve something

republic form of government in which the people elect their leaders

Roman Empire ruling power over much of Europe and Africa lasting from approximately 44 BCE to 476 CE

sanctions punishment of one country by another country or organization, usually stopping one nation from trading with other nations

scrubland land that has only very small plants, such as small shrubs

sharia laws based on the Koran that describe duties and penalties for Muslims

terrorist anyone who seeks to achieve political goals through violence

unemployment number or proportion of unemployed people

United Nations worldwide organization that promotes world peace and social justice

unity agreement among people or groups

vegetation plants and trees

wadi dry desert ravine that only becomes a river temporarily when it rains

Western referring to developed countries, especially in North America and Europe, but also including countries such as Australia

Find Out More

Books

Lange, Brenda. *Muammar Qaddafi* (Major World Leaders). Philadelphia: Chelsea House, 2005.

Moore, Heidi. *The Story Behind Oil*. Chicago: Heinemann Library, 2009.

Morris, Neil. *The Middle East and North Africa* (Regions of the World). Chicago: Heinemann Library, 2008.

Sullivan, Kimberley L. *Muammar Al-Qaddafi's Libya (Dictatorships)*. Minneapolis: Twenty-First Century Books, 2009.

Willis, Terri. *Libya (Enchantment of the World)*. New York: Children's Press, 2008.

Websites

news.bbc.co.uk/1/hi/world/africa/1398437.stm
This timeline of Libya's history on the BBC Website is updated with recent news about the country and links to news stories.

https://www.cia.gov/library/publications/the-world-factbook/geos/ly.html
Up-to-date facts about Libya's land, people, economy and government. You can also compare the latest data about Libya to data from other countries around the world.

http://www.calacademy.org/exhibits/africa/exhibit/sahara/
Website from the California Academy of Sciences that includes views of the Sahara Desert as well as information on the Tuareg.

www.historyforkids.org/learn/islam/religion/
Information on the history of **Islam**. This site also has other sections, including African history.

Further research

Most people will not be lucky enough to visit Libya for themselves, especially as political turmoil continues to plague the country. However, you can find out more about this fascinating country by researching the topics listed below. Visit your local library or have an adult help you research the Internet for more information.

- North Africa and the Maghreb: the countries of North Africa share much of their history and culture. Find out more about Tunisia, Algeria, Morocco, and Egypt to discover the similarities and differences between Libya and these countries.
- Oil plays a very important part in Libya's story. You can find out more about where oil comes from and why it is so important.
- Libya's relations with other countries, particularly the United States and Europe, have not been easy in recent years. You can find out more about why this is. Although Libya has opened itself up to the outside world in recent years, this could still change in future.

Topic Tools

You can use these topic tools for your school projects. Trace the map onto a sheet of paper, using the thick black outline to guide you.

This served as Libya's flag until 1977, when Qadaffi introduced his own flag. The National Transitional Council reintroduced this as Libya's flag in February 2011. The three stripes each represent one of Libya's three major regions: red for Fezzan; black for Cyrenaica; and green for Tripolitania. The white crescent moon and star represent Islam, Libya's main religion.

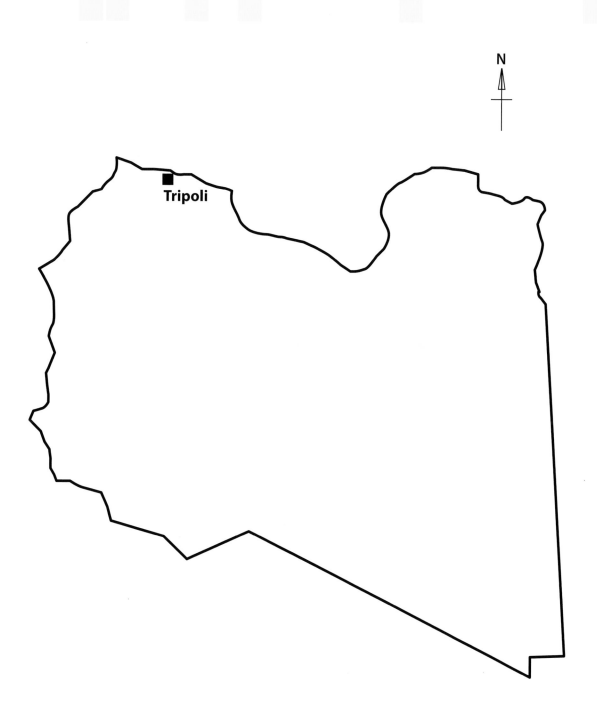

Tripoli

N

Index